Growing Up Pratt

A Memoir

by

Dr. Phillip J. Finley

Growing Up Pratt

First Edition, February 2011

Copyright © 2010 Phillip Finley

Cover Design and Book Formatting by Pedernales Publishing, LLC, Johnson City, Texas. For information visit www.pedernalespublishing.com.

Published by Finley Publications, Stone Mountain, GA. For information contact Finley Publications via email at phildr2008@gmail.com

ISBN 9780615445953

Printed in the United States of America

Sunflowers and Buffalo, a Black Kid's Story
of Growing Up in Pratt, Kansas.

By Dr. Phillip J. Finley

PREFACE

Pratt, Kansas is a small town that I grew up in. Even though I only lived in Pratt for nine years, for some strange reason, I cannot seem to erase the memories and events of growing up there. My grandparents, neighbors and class fellows helped me understand the importance of God, friendship, trust, and sacrifice. From Pratt I learned how to swim, hunt, fish, and build snowmen. I also became an athlete of sorts, and I attribute all of that to the rough play that my brothers, friends and I practiced in the backyards of Pratt. When I think of Pratt, I think of freedom; the freedom to ride around town on my bike, go to the movies, the park, and exploring. Pratt taught me to take risks, as a young black boy, and to understand that this world is just one big place waiting to be seen through the eyes of a child

Buster Browns

I owe my character, love of God, and love of life to growing up in Pratt, Kansas. The environmental area encompasses 7.5 square miles. The current population of Pratt is round 7,500 but I am certain in the mid 60s to early 70s the population hovered around 5,000. Despite its large size, it is difficult to fathom what beautiful people and experiences I encountered as a Pratt kid. There were the lovely snowfalls during the winter, my short walk from 720 S. Hamilton to Southwest Elementary School, the long awaited 4th of July fair, and the taste of sweet watermelons picked fresh from the Buckner's farm south of town. Halloween was not bad either. My family and friends would walk for several blocks or go to homes at the request of my parents, but the very last stop or sometimes the very first was always the popcorn balls up at Annabelle Bright. Here we would show up cold, tired, and awaiting a fresh hot popcorn ball.

We wore sneakers as often as possible and my mom would go barefoot throughout the summers. I do not understand why, and I do not recall flip-flops even being in existence and if they were, I never saw her wear them. As far as Annabelle's popcorn balls, my folks entertained a sense of frugality when it came to consuming one of those softball shaped, sugary morsels freshly made up the block. What I mean to say is that we would only get a bite or two per day. This treat would sometimes last several weeks maybe even into the Thanksgiving Holiday. Everyone in town, black or white, knew about the popcorn balls and often times you would find complete strangers showing up to get theirs.

Halloween candy was crucial to surviving Sunday School and morning church service. If I had not sneaked into the large paper sack (hidden by my mom) and scoop up some candy, it would have been difficult surviving those three and four hour services without an occasional sugar boost. I guess all of these events were necessary for the ongoing development of childhood; to follow the rules of our parents, respect our elders and be non-judgmental. There was nothing wrong with doing what you had to do as long as you were not caught doing it. Right now, I am picturing my mom catching me with my moving candy filled mouth. After the church services it did not matter if we had candy or not. Eating candy did not take away our appetites. We were always hungry knowing that when we left for church that morning, mom was preparing either a roast, baked ham, fried chicken, potato salad, green beans, rolls, lemonade, and her classic chocolate cake with chocolate icing including pecan pieces. A slow day would be pork chops. Cakes would last us about three days maximum, and if she did not have the time to prepare the chocolate cake, then it would be a lemon or strawberry cake that my Uncle Kent loved. Kent would prepare a cake from time to time. We always loved him for this because he did not hold back on the icing. My mom had to feed our dad, my Uncle Kent, and three sons and we were all energetic. My dad had a job at Luka for a while doing work at one of the grain elevators. He also did some construction work around town, but later he was picked up by Conoco Oil company as a roustabout. My Uncle Johnnie Hawkins taught him how to hang sheet rock, pour concrete, and paint among other things. My father was always a good man even before he became a deacon. I sensed something special about how he treated other people and how they treated him. Color did not seem to matter to him or those around him. His complexion is dark, and his encouraging smile and laugh invites those around him to become enveloped into his environment. I sometimes miss those days when my brothers and I would take turns doing the dishes, dusting, running the sweeper, arranging furniture once or twice a month, folding clothes, and preparing my dad's lunch for the following morning. My mom did not appreciate clutter. Though we did not have much, she cherished what she had and wanted it to last, so it was up to all of us to take care of the simple things that we were blessed with.

Pratt County was founded in 1876 by a gentleman by the name of Caleb Pratt who was a lieutenant in the Union Army during the civil war. Since then, Pratt has grown to be a major agricultural center for the state and the Union Pacific Railroad. After having grown up at 720 South Hamilton Street, we eventually moved up to 616 North Jackson adjacent to the Union Pacific Railroad Station. Although many people complain about living close to railroads, I do not recall any of my family members complaining about the noise. I attribute this to a strong and sturdy foundation and that we were sound sleepers.

Probably the worst part of living there was that our basement flooded several times. However, who was complaining when every morning you could smell fresh bread and donuts being prepared at Dillon's across the alley. There is nothing in the world like a fresh, hot, Dillon's donut. I am not a connoisseur of donuts like Kent Hadsell and my brother Craig, but there is nothing more delightful than eating a hot Dillon's donut; by far one of the best on the planet.

Other important events that were great in my life were the many movies and cartoons I saw at the Baron Theatre. I can recall a five-cent pickle, the ten-cent popcorn, a small drink and the large balcony overlooking the theatre. You could get everything you needed for your viewing pleasure for less than fifty cents, which was a lot of change at that time. Although many years have passed, the only movies that played there that I can clearly recall were the original Nutty Professor, the man called Flintstone, and Sinbad. There were other movies that I saw there. Today I cannot help but thank the management for allowing kids to go to the movies at such a small cost. On some days after the movies, a can of green beans or corn would suffice for us to eat that we purchased from the IGA across the street from Alco. I once recalled a conversation my father had with a group of people about Pratt. He said that what intrigued him about Pratt was being able to attend the movies at the Baron Theater without having to sit in the back or in the balcony. Since he grew up in the Jim Crow South, both he and my mom appreciated the freedom that Pratt brought us. Thanks to the Baron Theatre for becoming the selling point to one of Pratt's first Basketball All-Americans.

Little People

I have learned over the years that it is very important to have friends and associates. Most people cannot remember but I do recall the first day I attended Head Start. I do not have the exact address but I do know it was about a block from Main Street and a few blocks from Dillon, Oak or School Street. Not long after that, I ended up going to Southwest Elementary School to attend kindergarten. Though some kids would see this as a fun experience, it was a traumatic experience for me and the other little people. I wanted to go home just as soon as mother dropped me off. I did not understand why she would drop me off somewhere for a few hours knowing she was at home or shopping with her mother. I was still a little child and wondered why I could not just stay at home with her? Over time, I enjoyed attending kindergarten because we colored pictures, created pumpkins, made paper Christmas trees, Thanksgiving turkeys from our hands, and Valentines for our moms. Most importantly, we concentrated on how to color between the lines and not be messy. Sometimes I would even see kids that I went to church with walking in the halls while we waited in line for our drink of water and restroom break.

The coolest thing was having George Anderson come and help during recess. He would officiate at some of our dodge ball games in the gym. He was a good athlete and seemed to always have a look of a professional about him. He was chiseled, had a square face and from what I recall some amazing speed.

Anyway, we continued to glue pieces of construction paper together for whichever holiday was approaching. During Halloween the school would have a contest to see which class was the scariest, so we would parade around different classrooms in a line showing off our wares. We would also spend a considerable amount of time practicing our penmanship—big A little a. During the third and fourth grades, we were also learning how to count as well as having some major spelling bee competitions. This is sad but I have to tell you that the reason why my writing is so sloppy now is that I would rush through these training exercises knowing that lunch or recess would be approaching. After recess (in kindergarten) my mom would come. Sometimes I would be so worn out lying on my towel in our dark classroom that she would almost have to carry me out. I was always happy to see her mainly because in a few minutes I would be at home either playing with our dog Sparky or sleeping in my nice warm bed. This was a peaceful time before my brothers showed up. I guess that being away from your mother, having been on the earth for only five years, would be traumatic. One day you are being carried, kissed and hugged by everyone. Then all of a sudden you have to tie your own shoes, take a bath, and try to dress yourself. One minute you are being fed, and then you are told to feed yourself. Now I visualize myself in the room with several little people just like me, girls and boys whose level of patience were as short as mine and instead of expressing themselves by speaking would shed tears. After all, we were only three years removed from our bassinets. All of this was a part of growing up like the tall

Kansas sunflowers and baby buffaloes in July. Some of the little people that I presume were with me in kindergarten were Verlan Womack, both Marybeth's, Shawn Fleming, Cindy Swinson, Diana Mitchell, Cathy Brown, Dewayne Crockett, Debbie Kemper, and Doug Sims to name a few. I later hooked up with Joe Hit through Shawn and Doug. I miss these guys because one time I fell from the very top of Southwest's Jungle Jim, hit the ground and guess what my class fellows did for me at lunch? They gave me their portions of our favorite food; the biggest wheat biscuit and butter along with chocolate milk. There is something special about the way we were all brought up in Pratt. Age, color, religion, or political affiliation (whatever that meant at that age) did not matter. Once again, tears and not words comforted me, along with the heartfelt compassion of my fellow Southwest classmates.

Bless the Lord, O my soul, and forget not all His benefits.
—Psalm 103:2

Buster Brown Oxfords

I loved my grandparents. They did not have much, but it was their love they shrouded us with each time we visited, which was sometimes daily but mostly on the weekend. My grandmother would come by or we would go visit her every Saturday, so that my mom could get her hair washed, pressed, and curled for church. My grandparents did not have an indoor toilet or electric washing machine and dryer. It did not bother me that we had to bathe in a large bucket either sitting or standing depending on which area of the body my mom or grandma was trying to clean. What is so ironic about this is that when I lived in Nigeria for a few years as an adult, I realized this was a common practice. How could I have known that my upbringing was consistent with what was common in Africa? My grandmother and my uncles would spend a substantial amount of time out on the porch wringing their laundry through an old Maytag washing machine that I believe worked pretty good, and it did not matter what was the season or which clothes had to be cleaned. There were always creases in their clothes. The ability to look freshly polished despite economic shortcomings was also common in Africa and doubly important for being an African American. Our grandma's staple was rice and beans with pepper along with fresh green beans and a slice of bread, which is also still similar to West African dishes.

The best fishing I can recall when I was between the ages of five and ten was a small little creek out by the feedlot north of town. We would catch bullhead, channel catfish, bass, and perch from this little spot. We always used worms and bobbers and I do not recall a time when we did not come home with something

Thanks to my father, there was always good fishing out by Medicine Lodge. The second option would be the five-mile bridge.

To get to the Sawyer spot, you would veer off to the right when you hit the big turn north of town. I cannot recall a time when we did not catch some bass out of this pond. We never had to wait long to get a bite. By this time, my father had improved his game. He was now using stink bait, and would have at least two poles in the water at any given time. Fishing was serious business for him as well as keeping an eye out for snakes. To get to this spot, we would open the fence and immediately lock it up to keep the cows from getting out. The next step was to drive down about a half a mile and park. The biggest challenge was stepping over the fence to get there and taking a quarter mile walk down to the pond. My father and Larry Minnis made as much noise as possible along the way because they were more afraid of snakes than anyone on the planet and this fear has also been passed down to me. The thought that usually comes to mind for many avid fishermen are huge rods and reels, trucks pulling a boat, and the latest Zebco fishing accessories from the Bass Pro Shops. However, this was not true for us. We only had the bare basics and were successful at it.

My grandparents were working class people who scraped out a living through the sanitation department (granddad), odd jobs, beautician work (grandma), and selling chicken eggs. They also planted vegetables periodically; although I believe it was done to keep their minds occupied as well as to make a small profit.

Grandma kept a small change purse in her larger purse at all times, and it never seemed to be empty. Today most people would say we were poor, but I do not recall those words passing through my lips while I was growing up. I was under the impression that everyone was doing the same thing; ordering clothes and household items through JC Penny's on Main Street, buying sneakers from the check out stand at Dillon's, and eating at the local KFC on Saturdays, which is what my Grandma Brown would recommend when it was hot and she did not feel like cooking. Her chicken was just as good though. She was a slow cooker and now that I think about it, I believe she was somewhat of a perfectionist. She smoked cigarettes but never had a bad or unkind word to say about anyone unless she felt they were wrong. My grandma would often lie across her bed close to the window. With tweezers in hand and a large mirror in front of her, she would remove unwanted hair from her chin. The most comical part about her was a slight stutter when she got excited or mad at her kids—Kent, Kevin, or my mom.

When it came to our short fishing expeditions, my grandparents had a red late-model Oldsmobile and pick-up truck, which seemed to always have the hood up but was never parked for a long period of time. My grandfather could tinker with just about any engine to get it going, and he passed those same skills down to my uncles Kent and Kevin. My grandfather had been a mechanic and driver during WWII, so he had skills. Unfortunately, excessive alcohol abuse weakened his immune system. He passed away in 1975 at the early age of 55. His trademark calling to those he respected and loved was, "Hey Buddy." I have to tell you that on many weekends when my brothers and I would spend the night with them, we witnessed the painful and long-term affect of alcohol abuse which put him in such a stupor that my grandma would almost have to force feed him to help soak up the liquor that was in his system. She did her best to keep him in the kitchen, planted in a chair with a large spoon in hand to eat as much rice and beans as possible.

I can recall the vehicles back then having no air conditioning or seat belts. Both my grandparents enjoyed smoking and having an occasional Coors or Schlitz beer on hot summer days. Did I partake? Only when they turned their heads. My father once told my brothers and me that my grandfather, who was not a church going man, experienced something that changed his life forever a few days before he passed away.

He actually had the opportunity to experience a place most commonly known as hell. He told those around him before he passed away that he went to a very hot place, a place he did not want to return to. He said his feet and body were very hot. I miss my grandfather very much and I believe that God gave him a second chance; a chance to ask for forgiveness and to seek Him who created him. My father and other pastors prayed over him and I am sure he went to a much better place. He died peacefully not long after this. I know someday I will see him again and I will be there to call him my buddy.

The Brown tilt is the way that my uncles wear their hats, which was a trademark style and fashion statement that my father perfected. Every chance I get, I tilt my hat to the side in remembrance of my granddad, Mr. Leslie Brown. I recently spoke with my Uncle Kevin through Facebook and his take on his father's passing was "he did not know that he had choices." I believe that any addiction can be overcome as long as that individual receives support from friends and family, and if necessary professional help.

I am sure I will not be the first or the last to admit that I have had bouts with depression over the years. It is something that I would always try to shake off, but without having friends and family around for support through those rough times, you have to medicate yourself. I climb out of mine through running and thanking God as much as possible for what I have. I have lived abroad and I have seen how crippling life can be without 24-hour power, good roads, health infrastructure, schools, and a stable government. When all these things are lacking, you do not have much to live for unless God is with you.

Shopping was always fun with my grandma and my mother. Most memorable was the creaking floor at JC Penny's on Main Street. That floor would creek so loud, that even as a young child I could not run around and hide among the clothes racks no matter how hard I tried. This was a nice playground. It was here where we would pick up our catalogue orders. Though my mother would always lay down the law before entering every store that we had to be on our best behavior, it never failed that I would try to get away with as much as possible. I would act out and blame it on Travis Jr. or Craig.

My grandmother soon moved from her Ninnescah address behind the COOP Station, after granddad passed, to a small home on the corner of 10th and Jackson, which I believe has since been torn down. When we would visit, there you could always hear the constant sound of the power company across the street. During her remaining years, she traveled extensively with us to California, Washington State, Idaho, and all states in between. I have a very nice photo of me and my grandmother on the U.S.S. Missouri in Seattle, standing on the very spot where the Japanese surrendered to the U.S., marking the end of World War II. I also have a photo of her standing in the hills of Wyoming, in July, being showered by small snowflakes. Each state and every morning was an adventure that I know she enjoyed as much as we did. She never slept no matter how far we were traveling, and would request a coffee break every hundred or so miles. She passed away in 1983 at the age of 59. Grandma Brown enjoyed fishing, traveling, cooking, raising chickens and selling eggs. She loved her husband, kids and many grandchildren. She smoked slowly, ate slowly, could make a very nice apple pie that she cooked slowly, consumed her breakfast slowly and was just as comical and loving as anyone you would ever meet. At the age of five and six I looked up to her. She tried to exemplify how to treat others especially those in the white community. She made no apologies. Let us just say she did not rush that either. She loved to iron and made sure that her family looked fresh and crisp if they went out. That meant ironing handkerchiefs and undergarments as well. I would not say we were poor, but I would say that we were like many black families of the day. They struggled for everything they had, never asked for handouts, but were always willing to give what little they had to please others. I can recall older white and black men coming by to speak with my grandfather and share a small word or give him some fruits and vegetables from the local farms. If there was anything that was 100% with my grandparents that was clean, healthy, nutritious food fresh from the farm or from the chicken coop next to the house. The fried chicken she would cook could be smelled at least 50 feet away. Why my mother could not keep her hands off it I now understand. She would always use the excuse that the chicken was burning before reaching in and helping herself for a chicken thigh and drumstick and a scoop of freshly cut green beans and onions. Phenomenal food. The day she died, I did not know how to respond. I felt that it was not fair that she had to leave so soon. So many of my classmates had grandparents well into their 70s and 80s. Why did mine have to leave so soon? As a health care professional, I can clearly understand why. My grandmother had suffered from polio and walked with a slight limp. Having lived in Nigeria, I would say that despite the limp she was the luckiest woman in the world. I have seen men, women, and children move about on make shift carts with no use of hands and legs begging for food and money from morning until night. Though healthcare probably was not the best when she was born, she still was one hundred times better off than the hundreds I have seen who eat and sleep outdoors in the most remote parts of Africa.

Do good, O Lord, unto those that be good, and to them that are upright in their hearts. — Psalm 125:4

From a medical stand point, I would like to say thank you to Dr. Black our family physician and Dr. Johnson my dentist for keeping me alive and well. From what I understand, I almost died of pneumonia as a child. I do not know if it is true or not, but apparently Reverend Johnson and many others prayed over me. I was in pretty bad shape. I never had the desire to become a medical doctor, but I did receive my doctorate in health science from Nova Southeastern, Fort Lauderdale, Florida in 2007. My father was there to witness it, which was one of the happiest moments in my entire life. So today being one that is not quick to tell others that I am a doctor, I remain humble and continue to treat everyone the way my grandparents would want me to. I fight against but in every African country that I have visited as well as the short time I spent in India, I am referred to as Doctor, or Doctor Phil; not to be confused with the daytime TV personality. I learned from Pratt to be humble, express sincere thoughtfulness and humility in all environments and among all people. I know this sound like words of a politician but they are my words. I wore my Buster Browns with pants, shorts, and whenever my mom saw fit for me to wear them. They were classics.

Converse and High-Water Pants

What most people do not realize is that on Hamilton some of the best pickup football games in the county took place. The north sideline was Annabelle's, Billy and Tommy Bright, and the Campers. The south sideline; about 20 feet away I believe was a corn or alfalfa field. All

I remember was that very few passes were dropped out or inbounds. It just did not matter where you caught it. The older guys would always say something encouraging. Some of us would bump into parked cars, fall in the ditch, or get laid out by some serious blockers. Big Rick, the Martins, Andersons (Bubba), Morris's (Ted and Stanley), Brights (Kevin and Ricky), Flemings (Shawn, Van, Martin, Brad), Minnis girls (Leeann and Tracy), the little Finley boys, and others held their own on weekends or weekdays. You can walk up to any African-American male and some women and they will show you some sort of scar to prove that Hamilton was once a dirt road and the Infamous training ground for future stars. I attribute Kevin and Ricky Brights success on the football field to our games on Hamilton Street. My brother Craig who ended up as a running back for the Great Bend Panthers and future Langston Lions Football and Baseball star. As for me, I played basketball for several years in Duncan, Oklahoma, started on our Junior Varsity team, played baseball, and in April 2000 and 2001 ended up running in the Boston Marathon. Hats off to Hamilton. The girls were equally successful, Leeann became a major homerun hitter in softball and Tracy wasn't too bad either. George (bubba) and Robert both became outstanding football players for the Greenbacks. Travis Jr. ended up running track for Great Bend High and became an excellent sprinter. Did I mention he could dance too? This guy would compete against a guy by the name of Amador (last name) and would either win or be runner up. These guys could really move. Travis Junior would purchase vinyl records every weekend from Alco. At that time, they would cost less than a dollar.

You could probably say that we developed scars for fun without being scarred for life. Our scars made us strong. All I can say is that many of Pratt's best High School football and basketball players polished their athletic skills, Jim Brown moves, and Archie Manning double pumps right there on Hamilton, and yes the street does run downhill. If you cannot ascertain the full picture of these games, I can only tell you that the amount of dust that we kicked up, along with the Alco sneakers that we wore out helped define true athleticism, team work, and our way of forgetting the racial tensions in several southern states surrounding Kansas. Not only racism, but also the war in Vietnam, which lasted from 1955-1975. By 1974, I was ten years old and was somewhat reserved and protected from international politics. I do recall a tipping point in my life when things changed almost over night. In 1968, when I was at the age of four, Dr. Martin Luther King Jr. was assassinated. At this point, I remember seeing my father's shotgun behind the front door and we locked it for the first time, which felt claustrophobic even at my age. I believe that the talks that occurred among black men at that time whether in Kansas or Alabama was perseverance, survival, patience, anger, togetherness, and prayer. Now there were two assassinations that drastically changed the direction and historical perspective of our current environment; President John F. Kennedy in 1963 and now Martin Luther King. We continued to play on in Pratt but never relinquished the fact that we had to be vigilant, prayerful, and supportive.

Know ye that the Lord He is God: it is He that hath made us, and not we ourselves; we are His people, and the sheep of His pasture. —Psalm 100:3

Growing up in Pratt during the early 70s was phenomenal. We had a black park, which is now called Lorene Minnis Park. Back then it was equipped with a 2-4 foot deep swimming pool. Kevin Bright would purposely overflow it before his boss came around. We had one of the longest slides in the city that you would not want to slide down during any Kansas summer. This thing was metal. Need I say more! I remember straddling the edges and still burning my thighs on the way down. We also had a softball field, which allowed everyone of all ages to come and show off their hitting and catching skills after church or other family functions. In Pratt, family outings were an important part of our lives. We did not spend much time inside unless the movie The Shuttered Room was playing and even then, folks would be too scared to walk home. It did not cost anything to come down to the black park to play ball, wax your car, or just listen to Roberta Flack, Isley Brothers, or Earth, Wind and Fire piping out of someone's car. Some folks even had portable 8-track players, which really changed the environment. In the late 1960s Marvin Gaye, the Supremes, James Brown, Aretha Franklin, Sam Cooke, and the Temptations transformed the international music scene, spoke to segregated audiences in the south, and brought forth integration in the north. I can still recall the large Afros, bell-bottoms, dashikis, and wide collars. I never could figure out why there was no toilet paper in the restrooms though.

Last of all, did I mention the cottonwood trees? It did not matter if you could hit 300 feet as 50% of the time your ball would end up spending 10 seconds up in the trees before it came down and yes it was fair play. So, the best hitters would sometimes end up on third base by the time the ball found its way out of the trees. Yes, I can truly say that small kids were at a disadvantage by hitting low. Overall, the main objectives of these games were to encourage winners in all children. Larry Minnis and my father never called anyone out. They enjoyed playing more than the kids did. Both my father and Larry played town team basketball and softball leagues for many years, which kept them active in the community and throughout Kansas. When they could no longer hit home runs, they became two of the best referees in the state. My father has a few photos from the 60s when he played at Pratt Junior College. The shoes he wore to get the job done and become one of the region's best all-time rebounders were white high-top Converse better known as Chuck Taylors. Many of his records still stand.

Stained Glass Windows

I have mentioned how important fishing was to me, but I could not help but mention the guiding light–yes the Spirit that leads me, the One who propels me to get up every morning despite life's pain and frustrations. He is the one who keeps me moving when I go for my long hilly runs under Georgian skies, and enables me to smile in times of trouble and heartache. There are times when I feel I cannot do anything to get ahead. Life keeps moving and wants to stay ahead of me no matter what, and if I am unable to keep up, I will fall flat on my face and give up. I turn to God when my faith is challenged, and the basic premise of my purpose driven life comes into question. Sometimes we get so much thrown at us that we are unable to understand what and who we are and what is the purpose of it all?

As I mentioned earlier, I am a runner, and have been running for many years. The courage to run came from the courage to stand up at Second Baptist Church and recite what we called "peaces" (poems) given to all of the youth to memorize and recite during Easter and Christmas Holiday services. Those peaces were so essential to the kids and the parents alike. The kids did not want to embarrass themselves, so as soon as we would receive our peaces, we would begin to start memorizing. Ms. Catherine, the church pianist, made sure we rehearsed several times before the major event. It seemed like the rehearsals would go off without a hitch. There were those who knew their lines up and down and those who did not, but they kept repeating what they knew, assisted by Ms. Catherine and with some chastisement and then a repeat on Christmas Eve. It just never made sense to me not to prepare and be at the mercy of Ms. Catherine and have all of these people looking at me possibly wagering to see who could pull it off.

Very often, my mom would make a deal with us. She would tell us that as long as we did not make a mistake we just might get what we desired on Christmas. What a deal! I believe she did it to save herself from being embarrassed.

So there I stood from the time I was six until I was ten, every holiday, beard growing (inside family joke), stomach growling, sweating, standing there in a new black suit, clip on tie, and hard soled leather shoes. Can you imagine getting up in front of hundreds of people (probably 50) in a clean and shiny cravats hair style, trying to remember everything on that little sheet of paper cut out of Ms. Catherine's book of poems?

Second Baptist "Stained Glass Windows"

Now was the time to rhyme well, look cute, smile, and sit down in two minutes. What a nerve racking affair, but what brought me peace was the stained glass surrounding the sanctuary. I would sometimes envision the sunlight peeping through early Sunday Morning and at night the glass brought everyone a sense of warmth and togetherness. From what I understand, that glass has been around since the time the church was erected. I am certain there are some heartfelt stories behind how it was purchased and for what purpose. It began quickly with my eyes glancing out over the many heads in the crowd, and then quickly falling down upon the other kids with their eyes rolling around and mouths moving faster than the speed of sound. Sometimes speaking too fast meant you had to say it all over again. Now the only thing to worry about was Santa and would he come through?

My brothers and I always did well and my parents always came through with everything we needed and more. I can recall Christmas at Second Baptist seeing the elders come through in their black suits (Henry Munger dressed the sharpest), work boots, red and black stocking caps and ties. Our Kansas winters were generally rough in Pratt, but no one complained. Large snow falls were expected which meant impromptu snowball fights between kids and adults alike. Snowmen were erected in every yard, and among the men, there was talk about the first rabbit hunt and knocking down some quail.

The Second Baptist Church that was adjacent to the park is an old church that has been meticulously maintained for the past few hundred years. I slept on my moms lap there almost every Sunday, presenting her with a warm stream of saliva on her skirt or blouse after the service. I was baptized there around age seven alongside two of my cousins Shawn and Van Fleming. I also attended vacation bible school there in one of the small rooms overlooking Main street and the church steps.

One thing about Sunday church service and being a little kid was that your attention span was really short. As I look back at the service, I recall a hard wooden bench and my mother saying Amen. The foot taps of black women throughout the sanctuary was somewhat hypnotizing. My objective was to get a good nap in and hope that I could position the heel of my size 4 Buster Brown shoes against the separation piece towards the middle of the bench. Then I would not have to worry about my foot slipping and my sleep would be more assured. What I am trying to say is that frequent restroom trips were essential. It was an event practiced by all kids. At such a young age the loud creaking noises of the wooden floor compounded by several wooden steps down to the basement killed time. If anything unusual was taking place while you were down there like a mother feeding a baby, or watching the elders prepare Sunday meals for the visiting pastor then a five minute bathroom break could easily be stretched to about 15 minutes. I always felt my time was my own as long as my brothers or my mother would not come looking for me.

I learned at an early age that where there is a will, there is a way and if you want to be somewhere you have to invent a way of getting there. I figured that vacation bible school was all I needed. That is where I learned about the apostles, Moses, David and Goliath, Samson, Daniel, and the three Hebrew boys who did not burn up in the fire. In light of this, I never could fully understand why Reverand Johnson who was preaching about love, peace, and forgiveness would get so excited that he would have to spend the last 10-15 minutes of his talk speaking loud, sweating, and getting people to agree with him. I thought Church should be more like school or Sunday School. I had this talk with my father once but I do not recall what his response was. Just think of all the biblical training, Sunday worship, prayer meetings and bible school. Sometimes my brothers and I would come to church on Wednesdays only because we had been playing down at the park and needed some place to cool off and to use the rest room. We just showed up sometimes not only because we did not have a choice, but also because all the kids throughout Pratt would participate. Having a solid belief system was essential to understanding the basic concepts of faith, perseverance, and hope as talked about by the apostle Paul. Faith was crucial for a young black child growing up just a few hours from the Oklahoma, Arkansas, and Texas borders where Jim Crow laws and the rights of young blacks were still being stifled by segregation laws, internal bigotry, and societal un-acceptance of race gatherings. I believe our friends, parents, and relatives did a good job of sheltering us from all that was going wrong just a few hours away.

In African American households in Pratt, we were not taught to hate or to segregate ourselves from other children, but to be cautious, patient, strong, and supportive towards one another despite race. The Black Power movement was alive and well. What most people do not realize, or fail to realize, is that groups like the Black Panthers did not promote hate or go looking to cause harm. This organization would provide opportunities, food, clothing, and instill a sense of self-pride for the black community. We are talking about a people who did not have the support from local law

Phillip, Craig, and Duney. Teddy and Stanley Morris kneeling.

enforcement, a people whose highest ambition was to work at the post office, be a fireman, or school teacher. Even these opportunities were not always available, not even for those who were the most qualified. In the late 60s early 70s we as a people were fully aware of the race riots in Detroit, Los Angeles, and Chicago. We knew that just a few hours away blacks still were not treated right despite the new laws protecting them.

An eye for eye only ends up making the whole world blind
— Gandhi

Pawhuska Oklahoma

Traveling to Pawhuska, Oklahoma seemed like a very distant place for me. We would leave Pratt as soon as school would let out at Southwest, and arrive in Pawhuska around midnight. My father's mother and step dad were beautiful people. My grandmother cleaned house for some of the wealthiest families in Osage County, and my step-granddad was a barber in downtown Pawhuska. My great-great grandmother Dilly Dangerfield grew up as a young slave girl in Oklahoma. I wish she was around today so that I could ask what her life was like and how she managed to survive seeing and hearing so much hate and bigotry. Ms. Dangerfield passed at the age of 88 with less than one dollar in her saving account. I still do not know how she was able to give each one of my brothers a fresh fifty-cent piece each time we visited along with our Sunday School lesson card that we would keep.

My father's church in Pawhuska was built by his father and brothers. It was a rectangular sized building with a dirt floor and bench seats. Each Sunday my cousins on Ray's side would be the choir and midway through the service you would see Ray and William slowly fall asleep, waking up just as the pastor delivered his final words.

My cousins who lived in Pawhuska and Tulsa would always say yes sir and no sir. My brothers and I knew respect but we did not use all the southern formalities that were practiced at that time. We would just start talking or make eye contact. These formalities were new to us. Do not' get me wrong. We were respectful, but we would never say or do things that we did not feel emotionally.

Pawhuska was a fun place for my brothers and me to throw rocks, get chased by hogs, and swing on the swinging bridge. The difference was that we were always surrounded by blacks in Pawhuska, hardly ever seeing a white face unless we drove downtown where everywhere we would go people would acknowledge my father, or when we visited my grandpa Jack at the barber shop where he cut hair. We were always surrounded by cousins from two of my father's brothers. We would play football, tag, and softball. Sometimes we just sat around and laughed so much from the humor of Ray Jr. William, Morris, and Dean that our sides would just about burst, and this was without Jessie Dawn being around. If he showed up, forget it, as this guy could very well have been the Chris Tucker of the 70's.

It was always sort of a sad time on Sunday because we knew right after dinner we would have to get back in our station wagon and head back to Pratt. I would be so tired that I would not wake up until I felt our vehicle going over the railroad tracks on the south side of Pratt and then the rumblings of the red brick underneath our tires was an indication that we would be home in about five minutes.

In Pratt, we generally played and socialized in settings that were more environmentally convenient because of our small population. We had limited problems socializing in

31

grade school, but there were occasional fights that would bring our mothers to the principal's office to discuss what went wrong. Mr. McCall was our principle at Southwest and I feel that all kids looked up to him because he treated everyone fairly no matter what race you were. He would play with us during recess, and assured our parents that we were good kids. As we were a small minority, black mothers whether related to us or not kept a close eye on the youth, mainly because we did not have a voice to protect us in the event of any unlawful altercations. Though Jim Crow laws and blatant racism were not the norm in Pratt, television, radio, and news media painted a different picture, which added to the social delusion and question of what if.

The Second Baptist church was a social scene and a place for teenagers to hang out and talk. During the summers, it was not uncommon to see a few groups of kids sitting on the steps socializing and planning on going to Wichita or Hutchinson for a party. I only looked on because on days of communion my brothers and I along with Teddy Morris would drink the remaining juices from the communion tray but do not tell anyone that the mothers made us do it.

Mission Impossible

Believe it or not there were some summer mornings when there was not much to do in Pratt but find a buddy or two and ride bicycles, walk around town, go to the library or go down to Lemons Park. One morning my brothers and I met up with Cecil Fellows and I do not know why or how it was planned, but we did have in our possession some potato chips and pastries. These were pastries that were thrown away that our grandfather would retrieve and set out on our back porch. We had these things but no water. Today everyone carries water, but as kids, we would dangerously go hours without water. Our mini-expedition was to go down to Lemons Park to hang out and so with food in hand and no water we set out. It took about 10 minutes to walk over to the park from Ninnescah. The first place we went to was the lake over where the dam is. We stepped down onto the lake and made it over the dam and stood and played for a while. At some point someone gave us a stringer full of carp that we proceeded to carry for the duration of our mission. Somehow Cecil was convinced that this was good eating and I know some families would agree, but I was taught that carp were too boney and too much trouble to eat so we never ate them while we were growing up. As we took turns carrying the fish and following the small stream in the back of the dam, our fearless leader Cecil Fellows kept the momentum high and our mission essential. At one point, we came down a small hill in the woods and lo and behold, a large deer stood no more than 10 feet away from us. We were all frozen stiff knowing that an animal this size with antlers this large could kill one of us. Within a moment, this animal took off running in the opposite direction and Cecil gave chase with large Bowie knife in hand with intentions of killing this beast. We quickly followed and within a few seconds, the deer disappeared into the unknown. For all I know today he could have been behind a tree laughing at us, or halfway to Sawyer. After several hours we eventually came out near the five mile bridge, fish hatchery, turned South and wound up back near the pond on the South end of Pratt.

I do not know how this happened and since we were kids, we did not think much but just acted. As I am writing this, I am picturing all of us now wading through the snake infested Ninnescah River heading back into Lemons Park which would bring us closer to home.

Throughout life, we think back at the many occasions of when no harm came upon us and we knew that the good Lord was protecting us. I firmly believe that guardian angels play an integral part in protecting us when our parents are not around. From previous readings I have learned that there are approximately 8,000 snake bites annually each year and that the majority of deaths are to children bitten by venomous snakes.

A second point I would like to make is that being the youngest boy in this group of four, I felt I had something to prove. I had to prove that I was big like them, could do what they could do, and that yes, even though I was called the baby boy, sad eyes, sleepy head, or Pill-pill, I could hang. This was the tipping point, as Malcolm Gladwell would call it. We had to go into the river not knowing the depth or where it would lead. If you have ever spent anytime following rivers, you would know that cattails, tall weeds, and trees are part of the scenery. Generally, there is not a sand bank. If you have to venture out it would be a good idea to know the depth of the water, where it leads, and what species of snakes and other creatures might exist in unclear water.

We had all passed our swimming tests as boys through the red cross (at the big pool) so that also increased our confidence level for meandering into rivers and across streams. We had also swum in lakes and ponds before, so we were not afraid of what might be around. As a reader, you would probably think or guess that we encountered a fresh water crocodile, a school of piranha, or water moccasins while making our long trek through the river, but we did not. The moral of the story is that we had each other and we had a mission and that mission was to cross that river.

Looking back, I believe we were tired having traveled all the way out to the five-bridge during our adventure, over to the fish hatchery, and back into Lemons Park. Though we went unscathed, there was a price to pay. We lost the fish during the deer chase, potato chips, and other food provisions were either eaten or lost. There was nothing to do but walk slowly home all the while looking at the peacocks on the edge of the park. I am not 100% sure but I think Craig had slipped and dropped the stringer into one of the streams while in pursuit of the deer.

What I enjoy most about this experience and why God will not let me forget it is because living in Pratt gave us a sense of freedom to move about the community and explore new things no matter how silly or dangerous they were. Today you hear reports of black children who have lost their lives because they could not swim. All I can do is shake my head and thank God that at such a young age we all had the courage to do the unthinkable.

I carried my little red cross pen around with me for many years before I lost it. I used to attach it to my swimming shorts. Now that I am grown, I have nervously climbed into cabs in countries where people do not speak English. I have eaten foods that I know have not been refrigerated, selected meat from open markets where the butcher and his carcass are both covered in flies. I have ventured upon the highest roller coasters, slid down the highest hills on my snow sled, and climbed amongst the tall cottonwood trees at the black park.

Did I mention I used to play under the bleachers out at Pratt Juco? I could get away with it because my Uncle Johnnie Hawkins was the custodian. He was the guy who would sweep the floor at halftime as well as keep the Juco looking and smelling fresh throughout the year. He was a master carpenter who actually taught my father all there is to know about sheetrock and painting. As a little boy, I suppose I just could not always keep still, and always wanted to try something different, ask questions, and just be a happy kid.

At this moment, I am in New Delhi India contemplating my 14th marathon. I want to run a downhill marathon to increase my chances of qualifying for Boston again. I will need to run a 3:30, which is doable, but I need to get my speed back through our fall racing season in Atlanta.

Before I even think about doing that, my wife and I have to go river rafting this weekend in North Georgia. We just survived "zipping" about a month ago.

I now wear Asics Running shoes, which last far longer than the Dillon's sneakers my mom, had purchased for us back in her day. I recall them lasting no more than a few weeks. This should not be a testament to the quality of the shoes but to the amount of playing we did throughout Pratt.

Black Galoshes

This portion of my book may be taken out of context, but it is something that truly happened to the congregation at second Baptist church when I was a young black boy. One fall day a white man came to our morning church service passing through on his way to Africa, he said. This man who was in his early to late 40's said that he loved God, enjoyed worshipping with us, and would like to perform a favor for us if we would trust him.

After morning service, we all gathered in the basement, formed a semi-circle around this man and allowed him to show off a few African artifacts, pictures, woodcarvings and material that he had somehow collected overseas. He used the photographs as a template for the congregation to place orders, which in turn he would bring back within the next few months. My father and a few others gave this man money for masks and materials but unfortunately, we never saw him again. He expunged approximately $500-$1000 from the church that day.

When I reflect back on this experience, I cannot help but thank God for having given me and my family the opportunity to travel which has helped us better understand our environment and the uncanny behavior of people. I am not saying that I will never be taken again because I was at a mosque in Egypt where a man showed us around for about 20 minutes. After the fact, the Egyptian pounds that I handed him in one hand somehow entitled him to take as much as he saw in the other. All together, it was about $30 but it is the principle of the matter.

Though we may know Him by a thousand names, He is one and the same to us all —Gandhi

Christmas in Pratt

We got our fair share of ice and snow, which was the perfect backdrop for a white Christmas and a Happy New Year in Pratt. The red brick streets in and around downtown would turn into a white snow-filled canal with mountains (wind drifts snow, shovels pile it) of shoveled snow between parking spaces and parking meters. Reflecting back at Dillon's, I recall the snow shovels creating 10-20 foot piles in the parking lot. These piles would stay for several weeks before melting.

I miss the candy canes hanging from the light poles on Main Street, Christmas tree decorations in the windows, and large glass lights that signaled the beginning and end of the holiday season. There is nothing like seeing heavy snow and beautiful Christmas lights, strolling hand in hand.

Who could forget when Santa would come through the church on Christmas Eve and hand out brown paper bags full of apples, oranges, peanuts, and peppermint candy. The fruit was always really cold because they had brought the boxes up from the basement where they were prepared and stored in brown paper bags. It was something we all looked forward to getting. It was not uncommon for the deacons to give extra nuts and fruit to the elderly like Ms. McDonald, the Adams Family, and to those who did not attend church throughout the year. Was this a way of encouraging infrequent churchgoers to attend?

 I suppose but it was also a reminder to them that we still loved them and if they needed any type of support, we would be there to support them. Going to church should not be a prerequisite in serving humanity. That brings up important questions or concern as to why all blacks do not attended regularly. Was it because they had lost hope in the church, saw it as a money making opportunity for pastors, did not feel the need, or felt it was a hindrance each Sunday. Whatever the

case, it seemed like every Easter, Mother's Day, and each Christmas, the Second Baptist Church would be filled to capacity.

The Saturday before each Christmas service, all the kids would take part in decorating the tree. I can recall Charlotte Minnis, my mother, Ms. Catherine, Paula her daughter, Ms. McDonald, and Mrs. Adams and several Morris's participating in this event. We would pop popcorn, make long streamers, and glue red and green construction paper pieces together to make a chain to drape around the tree. The scent of a freshly cut pine tree could be smelled throughout the sanctuary. Santa, would position himself near our Christmas tree (white mask and white gloves) in the back of the church and he seemed to know all of our names, which was really cool.

Though I am 46 now and have a child of my own, I still believe in the magic of Santa and until this day I do not go through a holiday season without crying or going into a twilight zone trance thinking about my holidays in Pratt. I actually envision myself back in church during a cold Christmas evening sweating because I knew my time was coming to say my poem and once that was over I could focus on what was most important which was a Charlie Brown Christmas, Frosty The Snowman, and the Grinch Who Stole Christmas.

Travis and Johnnie

Here is a little bit about my mom and dad. My father was born in Pawhuska Oklahoma in 1940. One of five brothers, he was second to the youngest. Throughout the numerous visits to my father's hometown, I got a sense from friends and family that he was a pretty special guy. He was talented, popular, and his encouraging laugh and gift in speaking enabled him to later become an oilfield production foreman for Conoco, pastor of the First Baptist Church in Pawhuska, and the first black city councilman in Osage County. He grew up during the times of segregation. He used his athleticism to achieve all-state honors in basketball during all four years he spent at Booker T. Washington High School, and the now integrated high school in Pawhuska. I am sure many folks in Pawhuska only wanted to win and so they welcomed his skills as a basketball player, while others held on to tradition and kept silent. These were changing times where everyone would be treated as equal because it was now the law. While name-calling and threats abated over time, nonetheless any changes that give minorities equal opportunities is a slow process for both sides. Continual change propelled my father into basketball All-American status at Pratt Junior College. Offers came from all over the country, but for financial reasons he returned to Pawhuska and took a job working at the hotel shining shoes and doing other odds jobs. He was needed to help put food on the table.

My mother was a short woman standing about 5 feet 2 inches. She was born in 1942 and because of her skin tone, she was often times mistaken for Spanish and other nationalities. She had no patience when it came to foolishness and did not hedge or see things in grey. It was yes or no, black or white, eat this or do not eat at all. She was so loving/ abrasive at times. She referred to all the men in the house as "boy." Come here boy, eat this boy, give me the keys boy, clean the house boy, let's go boy, so on and so forth. She had good street smarts and had a keen view on what it took to raise a family. She simply utilized her survival skills day after day. I believe that she became outspoken because she grew up poor having lost a baby sister at a young age and having a father who abused alcohol. She fervently loved her two brothers and seemed to be the guardian of the family and a strong advocate for what was right. Unfortunately, through all the love and joy that she gave, she also endured a lot of pain and heartache having lost both parents and two sisters at a young age. She did not graduate directly from high school, but later received her GED from Barton

Travis and Johnnie; 720 South Hamilton, Pratt, Kansas

County Community College in Great Bend. She spent several years as a nurse's aide at Pratt Community Hospital working nights so she would not have to worry about child care during the day for three boys. Donnell my third brother was born in 1976. I was in the fifth grade at that time. My mom had many friends and associates, but her best friends while growing up were Charlotte Minnis and Joan Williamson to name a few. My aunt Dorothy Mae and Grandma Brown shared a closeness and a bond with my mother that I am now beginning to understand. As a black woman growing up in the 50s and 60s seeing, hearing, and experiencing what they did gave them the uncanny ability to assess family issues, racism, and what it took to be strong in an environment that was created to watch them and their families fail. I commend all black women that grew up during those times because they chastised all kids, kept us thinking straight, and provided the gift of love and laughter.

I loved my mother dearly and I wish I could sit down with her right now with a cup of coffee and have her console me, tell me everything will be okay, and that God is truly there to watch over each and every one of us. I want to know from her that the things I think about today are normal and if the pain and doubts that wonder through my mind are normal. I want to know how to be a better person through patience, faith, and to feel once again that no matter what I have done in life, no matter how bad, that she still loves me. Lastly, I want to feel and hear the silence as it leaves her voice, and feel her eyes study me, so I can feel proud again to be a part of one who loves me unconditionally. I want to learn more about her upbringing and what shaped her political, religious, and social values. I want to know what made her laugh and what made her cry. I want to go to Braum's again hand in hand with her, eat a hamburger and fries, and watch her spill ketchup on her blouse. I want to laugh and talk about women and watch her catch me blushing. I want to lie down next to her in bed and tell her all about my experiences in school, living abroad, and my life with Fauzia. I want her to know that my faith in Christ is as strong as it was the day I got baptized in Pratt in a white choir robe. I want to tell her how my daughter one day said she wanted to be baptized.

I punish myself because I should have taken her to the hospital when she fell in Kentucky. One week later, she passed away. I would like the opportunity to say goodbye to her and ask her if I could have done more. Most importantly, I would give anything to see her smile again.

As far as school goes, I honestly believe my mother had to prove something to herself, and to her father she had lost. She was compelled to do something rewarding and special in her life and that is why I think she returned to complete something that she was so close to achieving as a teenager. She also had four boys at the time and so this was the tipping point in her life; the chance to exemplify those who want an education should not have to wait so long to achieve it. They should do it when their heart is telling them to.

Reflecting back on my mom's accomplishment, this was a special occasion for her and if I had to do it all over again I would have known what that meant to her and provided all the love and support I could. However, as a young boy my only concern was when I could quit my paper route and find a way to survive each and everyday at a predominantly all white elementary school. Despite my selfishness, I could not have asked for a better mom. She made me chicken noodle soup when I was sick, taught me to tie my shoes, held me while I slept in church, supported me throughout high school, encouraged me at Oklahoma University, and loved to see me run.

People might not get all they work for in this world, but they must certainly work for all they get — Fredrick Douglas

Since the1960s, I assume that the gallons of milk my mother purchased from the farm near the cemetery were closely examined and that the processes used were the best around. In fact, the QA QC must have been good because I do not recall ever getting sick from drinking milk in Pratt. It was always a joy to watch the cows being milked behind the glass. Milk was generally the last grocery item that my mother would purchase when we would go shopping mainly because it was cold and we wanted it to remain so instead of sitting in the car on hot summer days. I recall shopping more at the IGA than from than Dillon's, no doubt because of our family size and the lower prices at the IGA.

What I did not realize when I was growing up was that I was surrounded by people who made up a family or village in African terms. These were the people who did your hair, gossiped, and drank coffee with you on the weekdays when you just wanted to get out of the house. The village women did not speak much around us and sometimes spoke in code, whereas for the men it was all about baseball, football, and basketball.

Thinking back I remember all too well what kept my brothers and I occupied while we sat around and listened to the elders speak. We would play with any pets that were around and stare at whoever was speaking. This is probably why I find myself staring at people today. I am trying to get a sense of what they are saying and where they are coming from.

I have always been told that I have an uncanny ability to figure people out. Within a few minutes I understand their character traits and their intentions. Once again, these social settings were all about keeping the family name safe and ensured that the respect amongst other villagers remained intact. I believe what brought these women together was family and the fact that they all had kids about the same age. In essence, they had children all about the same time which reinforces the fact that African American women at that time still thought in tribal terms and about what was in the best interest of the immediate family.

There was nothing like going into Dillon's and having a fresh chocolate chip cookie given to me by Venetta Fleming. I was about six or seven and I could not see above the checkout counter. With a fresh cookie in hand and a dozen donuts in the shopping cart, there was no thought about eating healthy unless lunch was at Bites (the restaurant with the 15 foot high basketball goal). Although my mother would want us to eat lunch before having a donut, it did not always work out this way. Sometimes we would eat half a dozen donuts before we got home, but we would burn those calories by playing outside until the sun went down.

There was no such thing as video games, (Wii) and IPods, or personal cell phones. We played army, threw dirt clods at one another, played mainly football, and rode our bikes everywhere. If we were not riding, we were walking. Making long distance calls on our green rotary phone in the living room was done only on Sundays since that was the cheapest day of the week to make calls. Fuel at that time was around 49 cents a gallon, an expensive car was around $5,000, cigarettes 52 cents, and you could find bread, ten loaves for a dollar.

My brothers and I never complained that we did not have the latest Nikes because they did not exist yet. It was not uncommon to wear hand me downs especially sweaters, blue jeans, coats, and football cleats. At that time, I was the youngest and was always eyeing certain articles of clothing that I would obtain in about a year or so. There was no need to fret, as I knew they were coming my way either in one piece from Duney or in several pieces from Craig.

Another activity that small children enjoyed were various school field trips. We would visit the fish hatchery, library, fire department, state fair, Joy land, Wichita Shockers Baseball games, Greensburg's hand dug well, Dalton Gang hideout, Barnes and Bailey circus, Dillon's and Larned's home for the mentally ill. We just knew about it and it was always the butt of many jokes when it came to kids acting silly. All of these trips were learning experiences that broadened our knowledge of Pratt.

The holiday that really stood out was the 4th of July fair. Even at the age of 46 I can still smell the gun powder from the fireworks, I can hear the nickels and dimes hitting the drinking glasses we were trying to win, and of course, the smell of cotton candy and a 5 cent coca cola.

Great Bend

The transition from a small and family type of environment that Pratt had provided to a city at least five times that size presented adjustment problems for the 10-year-old child I was at this time. I had to adjust to feeling a more cosmopolitan way of doing things in the black community, and it took some time for me to adjust and once I did, I was "cool." The living arrangement with three brothers and a smaller home kept us all closer together. I continued to throw newspapers even though snowdrifts were over 10 feet high. By the time I reached home after my hour or so route, my feet would be so cold I could not move them. It was common to wear at least two pair of tube socks but even that did not guarantee you warm feet during a Kansas snowstorm.

I really missed Pratt. We had lived in two beautiful homes in Pratt but now we were living in a new type of home called a doublewide trailer. The trailer would arrive in two pieces complete with a kitchen, three bedrooms, two bathrooms, family and living room, plus a utility room. We moved this unit from the trailer park we were staying in to an acre lot around the corner.

I remember the week that they moved it, it snowed and a portion of our home had a few inches of snow in it. My father had a brick foundation poured, which stabilized the unit and made it look more like a house than a trailer. He poured a sidewalk, had a carport constructed, and we even had a go-cart track out in the back.

I still had the paper route. The Great Bend Tribune would arrive everyday around 3:00 or 3:30 in the afternoon about the same time that the Flintstones would be playing or G-Force, two of my favorite cartoons. I also played basketball and football. Even though I did not get home until 4:00 or later, my father or mother would be waiting for me either in the car or in my father's work truck, where they sat folding the papers and putting them in the bag. I still had to wrap them after playing sports, and walk with the papers to approximately 150 homes at the trailer park we had just moved from. I had to get those papers out in all kinds of weather. I would try for 5:00 p.m. because that is when everyone came home from work. To be honest, this was the first time I really missed living in a home without a basement. Since then, when purchasing a home, it has always been a requirement for me for it to have a basement.

During the summers of 1976 and 77, I slept a lot which is common among teenagers. My voice changed too. My grandmother said that it was part of growing up. She also said that the long white dry mucous stream on the side of my mouth after I woke up from each nap was worm juice. I do not understand that one, but I held onto that belief for many years. I must have grown four or five inches, equaling my two older brothers in height. As you can guess this brought on conflict. The best way I can explain this without attributing any biases toward my growth and athletic perseverance is to include a passage by W.E.B. Dubois who stated that "social change in sociology is the alteration of mechanisms within the social structure, characterized by changes in cultural symbols, rules of behavior, social organizations, or value systems." In other words, my evolution from a boy to a man changed the social structure of the environment that I was living in at that time. My hands and feet became weapons and my mouth was there to escalate any unwanted social barriers that might be a hindrance to those around me.

Though I was no longer the baby of the family or the third Finley boy from Pratt, I developed into something that only God could imagine and that was a young black man with ideas, a curiosity for girls, sports, and the outspoken tongue of my mother, patience of my father, and a joy for learning new things. I missed Pratt though. I missed my church where I was baptized, the fishing holes where I caught my first bass, my uncles and cousins, Aunt Dorothy Mae and Johnny Hawkins, but most of all I missed my grandma who I knew was alone now with her youngest son, my Uncle Kevin.

As a kid, I could tell they did their best to survive. Kevin was a very active teenager who would work at odd jobs but find himself periodically in trouble with Pratt law enforcement. I do not know what it is, but I could guess that the reason why many of the young black men who lived in and around Pratt were sometimes found to be in trouble by the law was that they were the silent minority. They dated white girls, and though interracial courtships were just gaining a foothold throughout the country, being black, doing the same drugs as your white counterparts and dating white women sometimes did not go to well in the eyes of law enforcement and others throughout the community. It is just my thought. I am certain that everyone from the Wrights, Flemings, Andersons, Fellows, and Browns families could each attest to some negative situation that might have occurred whereby they were wrongfully sought out. Despite this, I always would see my uncle and other young black men with whites; partying, listening to music, or en-route to a party. The biggest thing to have in Pratt during the early 70's was a car as you can probably guess. Now let your imagination run wild on a hot summer night listening to Sly and the Family Stone, Three Dog Night, Roberta Flack, James Brown, The Doobie Brothers, Aretha

Franklin, John Lennon, and the Rolling Stones. A recipe for a good time was Earth Wind and Fire, and a bottle of Boones Farm, which I would rarely find under my Uncle Kent's bed when I would snoop while he was at work at Dillon's.

Socially Unaccepted

The friends that I thought I had were true friends. The friends that I wanted to be friends with were not. I once knew a guy that I would play basketball with periodically, and was later asked to spend the night at his home. This was a very new experience for me, so I did not know what to expect. Though I had experienced name-calling and bigoted comments throughout my fifth and sixth grade years at Jefferson Elementary, I did not expect to have my so-called friend request to go through my sleeping bag as if I stole something. He said his mother told him to do it. A few minutes later we went off and had donuts. The experience though is still fresh in my mind, mainly because I was ten and at that age, you begin to look forward in life more than behind you.

Your friends and families are telling you that you look like your father or mother, you have put on weight, begin to lift weights, or you have grown a few inches. So you enjoy the changes that are taking place such as peach fuzz on your face and other places, voice changing, and girls liking you. I believe I developed and learned instinctively from my mother about how to treat people and this was no way to treat a friend.

After that weekend, I do not recall ever sleeping over with him or inviting him to my house for anything. It is not that I was angry, but I was hurt because then I understood that events like this did not affect other kids my age. Just because I was perceived as a working class child from a black family meant that I did not have as much as he did. This meant that he and his family had sort of a feeling of entitlement. They were entitled to treat others lower than them as they pleased.

Dr. Martin Luther King wrote that "nonviolence is the answer to the crucial political and moral questions of our time: the need for man to overcome oppression violence without resorting to oppression and violence. Man must evolve for all human conflict a method, which rejects revenge, aggression, and retaliation. The foundation of such a method is love." Nobel Prize acceptance speech, Stockholm, Sweden, December 11, 1964.

My father was not home every day at 5:00 p.m. He worked hard to scrape out a living for a family of six. Probably the most interaction we had with him was on Sundays, while my mom did her best to keep three fighting boys from turning the house upside down the rest of the week. As I think back, it was pretty hilarious. Here you have three boys ages 10,12, and 14 respectfully, full of testosterone, living in a modest but small doublewide trailer, and trapped during the Kansas winter months. It was futile to attempt to keep the house quiet while my mom was expecting, sleeping, or just being mom.

What I thought was funny was seeing Craig and Duney flying over the kitchen table, kicking over the garbage can, and my mom trying to beat them with a broom but having no affect whatsoever. The whole time I was trying to see who would be my ally for the next battle that would take place in the next day or so. Nine times out of ten I would ally with Craig because he laughed while winning these altercations, and I did not understand Duney and though he is fifty now, I have yet to meet anyone like him domestically or internationally. Though we still argue and disagree, I still love him because he is my brother.

Growing up as a child, my father was a great provider. He bought me a go-cart, ten-speed bicycle, took my brothers and me hunting, fishing, and numerous vacations across the country. Some of the highlights were going to see Wilt Chamberlain, Jerry West, Phil Ford and Sam Lacy play in Kansas City. I saw George Brett and the Royals several times and we visited at least ten baseball parks throughout out the country. Mount Rushmore up in the Black Hills was memorable as was Washington D.C. and New York City. It amazes me when I look back at the photos of the twin towers. I thank him for showing me the importance of never quitting. I always imagine him coming home after dark walking across an icy carport with a lunch pail in hand, cap on his head and a big smile. Even though I wrecked my go-cart a few times he did not ask how it happened. He just repaired it, stood up and proceeded to burn our garbage, feed our dog, and pick up around the house. As for the go-cart, I chose not to ride it as recklessly as before.

Even today, my father does not worry much and if he does, he does a great job of not letting it show. My mom knew when he was worried because he would shut down (like I do today). He would get away and go fishing or need to take a family road trip to clear his head. I appreciate his character, patience, and his love for us.

I attribute many profound moments to my parents for being there when I was irresponsible and did not understand the big picture. I once told my father's congregation in Pawhuska of how he visited the Dean of the Arts and Science Department at the University of Oklahoma (OU), when I was placed on academic probation. My father did his best to listen and vouch for my character as a hard working son he did not want to be cast out of Oklahoma's most prestigious academic institution. To make a long story short, I ended up attending Rose State College in Midwest City the following semester.

The image that I will always hold on to was the tear I saw my father wipe away as we drove back to Moore, Oklahoma where we lived at that time. I knew then that I did not understand the big picture and if I did not shape up soon I would blow it. The weekends I spent drinking, or taking a hit or two had come full circle.

I had worked 30-40 hours a week at Pratt's grocery store and later Albertsons in the produce departments. As you can imagine there were days that I was expected to be in at 5:00 a.m. to break down the entire produce counter for cleaning. I was late a few times, but never called out sick. My mother at that time was disappointed as well, but she kept it to herself. One thing that I appreciated about my mother and father was that they knew that whatever I got myself into; I would find a way out. It never dawned on me that education meant so much to her and if I would have looked at the big picture I would have remembered what my mother went through to achieve her GED. I was able to raise my grade point average and re-enroll at the University of Oklahoma the following semester. I graduated from OU in 1988 along with my line brothers (Xi Delta Chapter, Phi Beta Sigma Fraternity) Dr. Kevin McPherson, Chris Dean, Anthony Rolfe, and Joe Hooks, "The sophisticated gents."

What I learned from this experience was that the parable of Christ about the prodigal son is true. My story unfortunately is no different from thousands of other young men and women who go about trying to find themselves in a world of temptation, peer pressure, and self-identity. In the end I had accomplished my goal of graduating from college, and though my life was compartmentalized into thinking that everyone knew what I was going through, it never dawned on me that what I envisioned as success may have been slightly different than what my parents thought. Just like the prodigal son my father was responsible for placing the graduation robe around me, and my mom told me that I should I place a gold ring on my finger, and new shoes on my feet. They did not kill the fattened calf, but there was a celebration, a celebration of life. In my eyes I survived, in their eyes I was probably lost, found, and alive again.

"For I know the plans I have for you,' declares the Lord, 'plans to prosper you and not to harm you, plans to give you hope and a future." —Jeremiah 29:11

Today's News

Here I sit at the Shangri-La Hotel in New Delhi India thinking about the past and why I am here today in one of the largest countries in the world with a population of over one billion people, on Krishna's birthday. I am among a nation of people who are polytheistic (belief in many Hindu gods), value family, and although poverty is a way of life for many I have never experienced such kindness and appreciation for the simple things in life.

The food is the best in the world for vegetarians and carnivores alike. As life and festive holidays occur all over the world, it is difficult to listen to the world events such as the after affects of the earthquake in Haiti, flooding in Pakistan, nuclear bomb threats from North Korea and Iran, raping of young women in the Congo, and the political filibustering going on in Washington.

We tend to want to find blame for our country's biggest environmental catastrophe in our history; the BP oilrig explosion that was impossible to cap for several weeks. There continues to be water shortages in many developing nations and rogue governments continue to turn a blind eye towards the people they were elected to serve. The poor are becoming poorer and the democratic philosophy of giving everyone the right to vote is becoming just that in many parts of the world, a philosophy.

People are hanging onto whatever belief system they grew up with and making it work for them. No longer do people believe that there is a way of life that can be fair to all because fraud and corruption has been so deeply entrenched into their way of life. They do not visualize another way. I celebrated with the rest of the world as the Chilean miners surfaced after months of being underground and yet we give more airtime to troubles of Hollywood celebrities. News channels and some newspapers continue to divide our country through the most simplest and antagonistic method of news wrangling, propaganda. It has taken the U.S. over 400 years to become the nation it is today and yet we try to push our free style economy in countries where it is common to overthrow government officials through coup d'état.

I was once told by a chauffeur in Africa that if politicians do not steal, that people would ridicule them into shame if they returned back to their village without substantial wealth, of course stolen from the poor people they were placed in office to serve. What happened to morality?

I assume that if it has not been taught, it will never be accepted as the normal way of life. What are the motivations of community officials to want to steal from their own people for their personal wealth and prosperity, while children a few hundred feet from their homes are starving and lack education. We have our first (not last) African-American President, Barack Obama. The world rejoiced but in less than a year of his time in office, people have lost hope because he is not working hard enough to turn around a failed global economic catastrophe. People feel entitled to say whatever they want about him forgetting what he has inherited, two wars and a failed economy, recession, foreclosures, bank closings, and thousands of manufacturing and technical jobs being lost to overseas countries like Mexico, China, and India. Our healthcare system is imploding due to the increased cost of basic health care. Health care reform, which will enable everyone to have health care despite his or her economic status.

I believe if we begin to respect and care for our planet, our planet will give us a surplus of the good things in life such as clean air, fresh water, and an abundance of food for everyone. We must not become desensitized to death and destruction, but ask ourselves why they are occurring and question what are the underlying motives for those in power to impose such strong regulations and policies over others. Genesis 1:26-28 says that man is to have dominion over the earth. We have a basic responsibility as short-term residents of this planet to take care of it.

President Obama announced a few days ago that the U.S. combat mission in Iraq has ended but we continue the fight in Afghanistan. Middle East peace talks continue. All in all childhood obesity continues to rise in China, Africa, Japan, and of course in the U.S. and diabetes is now prevalent in Ethiopia.

Public Health

I am not in New Delhi for a holiday but for work. As a public health advisor for the Centers for Disease Control, I have worked in several U.S. states, Africa, and I am now providing technical assistance to India's Global AIDS Program. Though I am only here for a few weeks, it gives me a unique once in a lifetime experience living on one of the largest continents on the planet. Since growing up in Pratt our world has yet to experience the vast amount of infectious diseases, poverty, lack of health infrastructure, religious conflict, government instability, and rights of women being systematically taken away from them because of laws created by man. This is common in countries like India, Africa, parts of Asia, and the Middle East. Since immunizations are not commonly practiced, the diseases continue to find hosts to cripple, paralyze, maim, blind, and kill millions. Infectious diseases such as HIV/AIDS, sexually transmitted diseases, tuberculosis, and malaria are a common way of life for many countries. Without basic health care, education, and training of health care providers, these diseases will continue to ravish the young, old, and poor communities.

Poverty is a way of life for millions who do not have the basic essential nutrients, or the availability of clean water to survive in spite of the fact that many of these nations are rich in raw materials. This only adds to the dilemma. Insects such as mosquitoes have caused malaria infections throughout Africa (3,000 children per day), India, South America, and parts of the United States. HIV/AIDS continues to be prevalent in South Africa, Nigeria, and India. Dengue is becoming more common and diseases like polio, guinea worm, and leprosy still persist. Now we prepare each year for the latest flu vaccine to prevent us from getting sick or possibly becoming one of thousands that die each year from the most severe flu cases.

Through the Global Health Initiative (PEPFAR II), and Global Fund, all countries are training and collaborating with ministry of health officials, local doctors, practitioners, nurses, non-governmental organizations, and local citizens to help identify, control, and eradicate infectious diseases. Since my childhood, I experienced the unnecessary or I might say pre-mature deaths of many friends and family members who died by way of HIV, diabetes, heart disease, sickle cell, high blood pressure, traffic accidents, and through old age.

In Pratt on hot summer days, my brothers and my friends used to turn on the water hydrant outside while playing. There were no reasons to fear tainted water, cholera, or other water-borne diseases. Now we drink bottled water, not by choice, but because in many parts of the world filtration devices are ineffective and, industrial growth of cities, states, regions or countries becomes more important than replacing aged sewer and water filtration systems.

We should never take sound and effective health practices for granted. Most importantly, we should continue to push parents, and our school administrators to bring back recess and other physical activity programs into the schools. Without these, we will continue to see increased rates of heart disease, obesity, and diabetes in children. Whatever happened to punt, pass, and kick (PPK) and the president's physical fitness test? Even if you were only slightly competitive, you would look forward to taking part in your physical fitness exam, which was climbing a rope, doing sit-ups, and running a timed 600-yard dash. If a child succeeded as my brothers did a few times, they would receive a patch, which meant that they had successfully completed the program.

Organizations such as the Food and Drug Administration (FDA) and the Environmental Protection Agency ensure that all food and water that we consume is of the highest quality. The highest quality meaning providing the tools to eliminate and reduce the probability of any bacteria, pests, and vermin that may come into contact with our food and water. Without strong regulations, laws, and policies and the ability to see these enforced and protected by the government, then some quality assurance quality control processes will become lax, possibly opening the window for serious diseases like cholera, food borne pathogens, and viruses that can cause serious illness, diarrheal infections in children, and possibly death.

Conclusion

Having grown up in Pratt, my only exposure to the outside world was what my parents allowed me to view in person or on television. Often times I would hear that certain friends and distant relatives had passed away, but it did not affect me much just as long as my immediate family circle was not affected. We were systematically sheltered from death and pain. This is probably the reason why I have such fond memories of Pratt because I did not experience the death of anyone that was in my circle until my grandpa died after we had moved to Great Bend. It was then that Pratt began to feel like a distant place filled with pain and loneliness. My mom had lost her father, my grandmother had her lost her husband, and my uncles needed guidance, the guidance they had acquired while I was growing up in Pratt. My Aunt Dorothy Mae and Uncle Johnny were getting older and my Aunt Ravenna and JP Neal were still around in Great Bend. I was sometimes inquisitive as a small boy so I am certain that I asked my parents to have my grandmother leave Pratt and come join us in Great Bend.

I recently read the book "Everything I learned, I learned in Kindergarten." So true. Some would say it is selfish to want to have my grandma around. Maybe it is, but when you have been taught to love and cherish special people who have made the biggest impact in your life, it is hard to let them go. Inevitably, my family left behind many good friends and family, and life's memories of Pratt are always a memory of smiling, laughing, learning, sharing, and some crying. I miss Pratt.

Profound Moments

- I love God first, and foremost.
- I have been baptized.
- I have a beautiful and healthy daughter.
- I have visited London
- I have visited New York City.
- I have swum in the Indian Ocean.
- I live in the city of Martin Luther King's upbringing and burial.
- I have visited John F. Kennedy's tomb and Daley Plaza.
- I have visited the Tomb of the Unknown Soldier.
- I have toured Washington, D.C.
- I have visited Fort McHenry (Star Spangled Banner).
- I have seen Abraham Lincoln's tomb in Springfield, Illinois.
- I have seen the twin towers and stood next to the Empire State Building.
- I have visited the Kings Mansion in Uganda
- I have visited the Gambia with Dr. McPherson and Chris Dean.
- I have laughed until I cried in Amsterdam.
- I have petted Cheetahs in Kenya.
- I have Run along the ocean in South Africa and stood at the Cape of Good Hope.
- I have jumped off the cliff at Ricks Café in Negril Jamaica.
- I have snorkeled in the Bahamas.
- I have been on Goree Island (slave fort) Senegal West Africa.

- I have been to St. Georges Castle in Elmina (slave fort) Accra, Ghana.
- I have been to Mount Rushmore.
- I have gone white water rafting in Georgia.
- While underwater, I was face to face with a Barracuda in the Florida Keys.
- I went up in a helicopter in Missouri with my father.
- I saw the Salmon run in Oregon.
- I was first on the scene and I provided care to a pregnant woman and husband who had just skidded off the road outside of St. Johns, Kansas after an icy snow storm. I do not know who they were.
- I have been called a nigga.
- I broke my arm.
- Spent the night at the Fulton County Detention Center
- I have seen the Grand Canyon.
- I have been to the Hoover Dam.
- I had lunch with my mom.
- I stood in front of Desmond Tutu's Home in Johannesburg, South Africa.
- I rode a train from Amsterdam to Brussels.
- I grew dread locks.
- I went deep-sea fishing in Florida and caught several groupers.
- I floated in the open market in Thailand.
- I lived in Nigeria
- I have been close to the Secretary of State, Hillary Clinton.
- I rode horses.
- I stood next to the Great Pyramids (Giza) in Egypt.

- I saw the source of the Nile.
- When I was eight years old, I jumped from the high dive at the big pool in Pratt (one of the scariest moments in my life at that time).
- I visited the Blue Mosque in Istanbul, Turkey.
- I saw the world's deepest hand dug well in Greensburg, Kansas.
- I shot 3 point baskets during a time-out at Market Square Arena in Indianapolis.
- I have been to Nelson Mandela's House in Johannesburg. South Africa.
- I visited Anne Frank's House in Amsterdam.
- I visited Prague and drank beer.
- I rode bikes in Berlin, Germany and drank some more beer.
- I have seen Antwerp.
- I have visited Brussels and witnessed the little boy "pis".
- I ran in the Boston Marathon twice; even appeared briefly on CNN.
- I learned about Christ through my father.
- I lived in Pratt.
- I bought candy at Bailey's near Pratt High School
- I have seen the Lion King, Romeo and Juliet, and Annie at the Fox Theatre.
- I have run in 13 marathons.
- I wear cowboy boots
- I have crooked teeth, big ears, and sad eyes.
- I have seen the Golden Gate Bridge and visited Alcatraz Island.
- I have run 208 miles with a team of 11 people across the

Blue Ridge Mountains.
- I was a Navy Reserve honorably discharged.
- I have been lost
- I haven't begged for bread
- I lived in Pratt near the Hot Cold towers.
- Been on the roof of Southwest Elementary – don't tell Mr. Hall
- I visited the Taj Mahal and Red Fort in India.
- I love my wife, daughter, parents, and brothers.
- Married Dr. Fauzia Khan from Lahore.
- I am highly favored.
- I miss my mom.
- Most of all, I grew up seeing Buffaloes and Sunflowers in Pratt

Why write about Pratt?

I was born in Pratt July 10, 1964 at Pratt Community Hospital. I have been told that my mother could not decide on a name for me to place on my birth certificate. A nun offered her assistance. She said name him Phillip Jon after the Disciples of Christ. So here I am, Phillip Jon Finley. I later added Doctor of Health Science after some soul searching and depression. Throughout my life, I have seen a lot but each time I travel, I always end up telling someone that "I am from Pratt, Kansas."

Like anyone that has been blessed and given the privilege to see what the Lord has made, one finds oneself happy, sad, frustrated, religiously inclined, doubting, loved, hated, ignored, and so you end up asking yourself, why am I here? Where did I come from and how will I contribute to society? All we can be assured of 2nd Timothy 4-7 when the Apostle Paul states, "I have fought a good fight, I have finished the race, and I kept the faith."

We are not all destined to be entrepreneurs or inventers. I have discovered that some of the most important people in life are those that have served mankind in some capacity: Mother Theresa, Mahatma Gandhi, Nelson Mandela, my mom, dad, step-mom, and Martin Luther King to name a few.

Giving back in a simple way to those who have nothing is a principle that all religions strive for. Our job in life is to do our part in eradicating poverty, providing fresh food, water, education, and shelter for the homeless. The foundation of humanity though is to provide the most basic essential health care needs for our women, children, and the elderly.

It is astonishing how the tides turn in life. In Pratt I was given the required childhood immunization shots, and dental care, yet was so ill at one point that I was near death. My life was saved by Dr. Black, our family physician who had, by the grace of God, the essential tools and the skills to serve his fellow human beings. Today, God has allowed me to do the same in his own special way.

I have been young, and [now] am old; yet have I not seen the righteous forsaken, nor his seed begging bread. —Psalms 37:25

11105051R0

Made in the USA
Lexington, KY
11 September 2011